A Child's First Christmas In Heaven

by

Barbara Geesey

A Child's First Christmas In Heaven
by Barbara Geesey

Printed in the United States of America

ISBN 9781615791996

www.xulonpress.com

Table of Contents

Preface

*This book is dedicated to anyone who has
ever loved a child...*

Everyone has a story to tell. Most stories are heart-felt and deeply meaningful. Some will stay with us forever.

This story is about a severely handicapped little girl named Ella. Yet, despite her disabilities, Ella transformed each member of our family into a stronger, better person. She was a truly unique and inspirational child.

Embarking on life's journey with a disability makes each day both harder and more precious. God has a plan for each of us, including those who are struggling with handicaps of various kinds. But when you look around, you will see signs of hope, wonder, and beauty – you just have to look for them.

When we consider life an adventure rather than a duty, amazing new vistas will open before our eyes. Gifts are all around, often in the form of friends and loved ones who offer their help and prayers along the way. We just have to make time to be open to the beautiful influences that appear in the unexpected twists and turns of the path we tread each day.

We must never take life for granted; it is far too valuable and brief. Even when the journey takes you where you never wanted to go, trust God's leading and watch for miracles to happen. They may not be obvious at first, but if you wait patiently, you will see him at work in your life and in the lives of those around you.

There are many handicapped and medically fragile children who need foster care and respite aid. When you open your heart to them, you may find yourself face-to-face with God's love and grace.

My First Christmas in Heaven
Mano-May Palmer, 1926-2003

I saw countless Christmas trees
Around the world below.
With tiny lights, like Heaven's stars,
Reflecting on the snow.
The sight was so spectacular,
Please wipe away the tear.
For I spend Christmas
With Jesus Christ this year.
I heard many Christmas songs,
That people hold so dear.
But the sounds of music couldn't compare,
With the Christmas choir up here.
I have no words to tell you,
The joy their voices bring.
For it is beyond description,
To hear the angels sing.
I know how much you miss me,
I see the pain in your heart.
But I am not so far away,
We really aren't apart.
So be happy for me, dear ones,
You know I hold you dear.
And be glad I spent Christmas
With Jesus Christ this year.
I sent you each a special gift

From my heavenly home above
I sent you each a memory
Of my undying love.
After all, love is a gift more precious
Than pure gold
It was always most important
In the story Jesus told.
Please love and keep each other,
As my father said to do.
For I can't count the blessing or love
He has for each of you.
So wipe away that tear and remember
I am but a whisper away from you.

Introduction

A Christmas Visit

Tom, our three daughters, and I stood on the crest of a small foothill in the Rockies on a crystal-clear day. Above us were the most beautiful blue skies I had ever seen; beneath our feet lay the glistening snow, as though a million tiny diamonds had been sprinkled across the cemetery in a fitting tribute to the fallen. It was December 24, the day before Christmas, perhaps the most hopeful day of the year, and of all places I was glad to be here.

On the hill's downward slope, patches of grass stuck through the snow in a determined effort to shake off the seasonal cold. But here on the pinnacle above the bustling mountain town below were the graves of several children. For a few moments, we pondered the tremendous joy and sorrow represented in the rows of stones all around, the lives of a family's child whose clamoring voice or excited whispers would no longer be heard.

Here was the headstone of Ashley, the talented young skier who had tragically died at age thirteen.

Brianna had been someone's beloved two-year-old angel.

Just beyond was the small mound under which reposed the brand new baby who had scarcely drawn a breath or two, whose brief life as yet was not commemorated with a gravestone marker.

A few long-lived pioneers of the town were buried around us, their stories, if not their names, already forgotten.

We stood before the headstone of our Ella.

We looked at each other, and then at the small, upright stone that stood as a lasting memento of little Ella, whose coming had changed our lives in unforgettable ways. Her passing had touched us in an even more substantial way. Who would have thought this young, disabled child could have left such a powerful legacy?

The brilliant sunlight grew anemic in the afternoon chill. The five of us clasped hands and murmured a final prayer before turning to make our way down the hill before the longer winter night overtook us.

I was the last to leave, following the others, ensuring they did not slip on the frozen snow. Taking a first few cautious steps, I turned for a last glimpse of my beloved Ella's resting place. She would have loved it here, the solitude amid nature's beauty. Somehow I knew she was not alone; I could feel her spirit, free of its bonds of clay, dancing in the breeze that sprang up rather suddenly. This was Ella's way of telling she was happy and at peace. There was no need to fear for her anymore. Ella had entered a new land of joy that no one could take from her. She would be celebrating Christmas in the best place of all this year. Someday we would join her.

Feeling the sun's warmth fade from my face, I blew a kiss to our girl and made my way quickly and cautiously after the others. Each person under those stones had a story to tell, if we only had time to listen. This is Ella P's.

Chapter Two

Empty Nesters

Raising three active girls in our hectic household over the span of two decades, it was with a bittersweet mixture of sorrow and relief that we helped the youngest prepare for college. I was almost used to the routine of sending them away, having done it twice before. Our daughters had been good students with high grade point averages, and they had been involved in sports, dance, and extracurricular groups. My husband and I had put in plenty of time driving them frantically from soccer practice to piano lessons, as well as sleep-over's with their friends and shopping trips at the mall.

"Ready for a break?" Tom had asked one morning over our morning coffee.

"Whew! I sure am," I admitted, glancing at the piled-high laundry basket that set before the door of the laundry room.

"It won't be the same without them comin' and goin'," he said, shaking his head. I smiled to myself, thinking how sweet it was that Daddy's youngest girl was moving away and he was missing her already.

In addition to raising our family, I had been teaching school for thirty years, and had seen more than my share of setting rules, issuing consequences, and offering rewards, as well as bandaging bruised knees and praising potty chair success. I loved kids – Tom and I both did – ours as well as my students. But we were also looking forward to having some time on our own for a change. After all, we were in our early fifties and still had plenty of energy and good health to enjoy the activities we had sorely missed while raising our girls: travel, date nights, romantic vacations. I had thought about training for a marathon or taking up golf again, though I would probably settle for hiking or biking new trails. It's not that we had never done exciting things – we had. But they had occurred few and far between the other stretches of time in which we focused on maintaining our home and cultivating a family life. By God's grace we had done a good job; the girls had turned out well. But now we were ready for something more…a change of routine.

I was a bit restless these days. After we had unpacked our daughter in her new dorm room, said our goodbyes and drove off, what would I actually do with myself? Of course, a few options had come to mind. I could continue teaching or donate my teaching skills to a short-term volunteer project, like teaching English to immigrants, for example, or join the Peace Corps. Perhaps I could even assist at an Africa AIDS orphanage. Tom was still working full-time, so he did not face the same dilemma as I did.

All I knew was that I needed a heartfelt change doing something that was meaningful. I prayed and pleaded for God's help in choosing a direction. As soon as I began praying for guidance, I knew change was coming. There had been other times in my life that I had sincerely prayed for something to happen – and the prayed-for situation had always fallen neatly into place. The signs could always be counted on to appear.

Oddly enough, I had started dreaming about babies, which I attributed to my daughters' coming of age and growing toward independence. Twenty-one-year-old Renae was a student at The University of Kansas, while her sister, Maureen, who was then twenty, attended Colorado State University. Our youngest, Courtney, just eighteen, would enroll at the University of Colorado, which thankfully was just an hour from our mountain home in Evergreen, but yet was worlds away from my everyday life. The girls no longer needed me, but maybe deep down inside I still needed them. I don't understand exactly where this feeling came from. All, or most, women are born with a strong maternal instinct that is hard to suppress or ignore. I had been so grateful to have children, when many women cannot, and not just one, but three. They were beautiful girls, inside and out. With God's help they had grown up to fulfill the promise of their potential, and my role had changed from center stage drama director to sideline coach, cheering and guiding the girls whenever I could. For the most part, they were self-sufficient. Yet, I knew there would be times when they would need me; they still had things to learn, and so did I. Our family roles would adjust, now that we all were older, but they would not end.

I wasn't ready to retire my skills and experience. Surely something more was in store for me, some plan or event in which I would have a stake or be able to help in one way or another. Maybe it would be a life-long change of direction, or perhaps it would be a series of brief, isolated events. I just felt that something was coming, something important and yet not life-shattering. God had been preparing me for many years to become a strong and effective parent through the experience of raising three daughters. It was hard to believe that all that acquired experience would now be stored away and remain unused. But without a clear sense of leading, I wasn't sure how best to apply my training.

But God had a plan. He was about to intersect my life with those of other people in ways I never would have expected. All I had to do was be patient and wait on His timing. Waiting is never easy for me, and I am not especially patient by nature. That is probably why I found myself in the position of waiting with uncertainty! Maybe I was preparing for an unknown future challenge, as an artisan prepares a piece of pottery for special use. My life was being molded and formed for utility, strengthened by fire, and then glazed to last.

Somehow, I knew I was waiting for something exciting that was coming down the road.

Chapter Three

Ella's Birth

It was about this time that a baby was born to a young family with whom we were acquainted. While we celebrated the advent of new life to this world, our hearts filled with sympathy for the parents and infant, as the tiny baby girl had been born three months premature with a tiny head and severe handicaps. She was precious and delicate, leading relatives and friends to believe she would not survive very long. The doctors, too, felt that the baby had a slim chance of living much beyond her first days. Everyone that heard of the situation grieved for the child and the parents' despair for her short life.

Tenderly embracing their newborn daughter, the young mother named her *Ella*, a feminine diminutive of names like Cinderella, suggestive of her fairy tale existence that promised to be much too brief, and Stella – Latin for "star," reminding us all of the infant's celestial origins and perhaps imminent destination.

Ella's impairments were many and complex. If she lived for any length of time, which her doctors felt was doubtful, she would require ongoing doctor appointments, therapy consultations, challenging and expensive treatments and medications, and round-the-clock care at home. Her parents heartbreakingly realized they lacked the skills to care for Ella's many needs. Feeling her time on earth would be short, they reluctantly decided to place her with an adoptive family with experience in caring for children like Ella. Surely her life, such as it would be in the short time left to her, would be in better hands with knowledgeable caregivers than two young unmarried parents who had no idea of how to take care of a child with multiple disabilities.

They contacted local adoption agencies, as well as church organizations, all of which were greatly excited to be offered a newborn girl for adoptive placement with one of the eager couples who desperately wanted a small baby to raise. The agencies courted the parents aggressively, promising a loving family and a smooth transition – until they learned that the baby was severely handicapped. Suddenly, no one returned the parents' phone calls. One agency did suggest that the family post Ella's information on the Internet to attract a wider range of applicants. Maybe they would be able to find any adoptive family that way. Apparently the locals had lost interest.

The doctors who had delivered Ella and monitored her newborn care urged the young parents to hurriedly make arrangements to put the baby in a foster home or give her to state officials for placement in a medical foster care facility. Some medical staff even suggested that the family stop feeding Ella and just let her pass away quietly, unwanted, unheard, unseen. The appalled parents sorrowfully watched their vision fade away of a loving, adoptive family arriving to embrace Ella in their family and provide her with the special care she needed for however long she lived on earth.

Then destiny brought our two families together.

I knew of the situation and was acquainted with the parents. Hearing that their child had arrived early and with serious disabilities, I made a point to visit the young mother and her newborn daughter in the hospital. I intended to have a cheerful visit, bringing encouragement to brighten the dismal outlook.

Elizabeth, the child's mother, looked pale and sad in her hospital room. Following her down the hall to the nursery, we peered through the huge glass window at a sleeping form in a bassinette near the window. I saw a beautiful cherub face with fuzzy brown hair nestled in the blankets. Then we returned to Elizabeth's room and I sat down while she climbed back into bed. Then we quietly ate the cookies I had brought. Thinking back on my own three deliveries, I remembered how tired I had been, and a little melancholy, which often happens after childbirth. Somehow Tom and I had made it through those sleepless nights and nerve-racking days with our eldest. Later, our second and third daughters had been easier to care for, though they still kept us hopping in a rigorous routine, as all babies do. Now, studying Elizabeth's slumped shoulders and rumpled hair, glancing around the untidy room, I knew she felt over-whelmed, so I was not surprised when she admitted her distress.

"I can't take care of her!" she sobbed, covering her face with her hands. "No one wants my baby, but I don't know how to manage anything."

Immediately I was at her side and hugging her as I spoke.

Almost without thought (except perhaps a subconscious idea that had begun forming), I spoke up:

"I will take Ella. I want her."

All I could think of was the baby's peaceful features and Elizabeth's huddled form. Surely this was the right thing to do.

It was. I had no later regrets. I have been writing Ella's story in my head since that day.

When I got home that afternoon, I told Tom and the girls about the youthful family's plight, and they were as moved as I had been. In unison we agreed to bring baby Ella home to live with us. It was sad that the adoption agencies had failed the young, needy mom and the unprepared dad. No one wanted to adopt Ella, so we would. I wasn't sure how things would work out, or how the decision would impact me personally or our family long-term. Somehow I just felt it was the right thing to do. Ella seemed to become "our" baby the first time I visited her in the hospital, just days old.

But now the real work of meeting her needs and providing quality care would begin in earnest. I hoped I could handle the task that I had taken on so precipitously in that forlorn hospital room.

Chapter Four

Bringing Ella Home

I visited Ella in the hospital each day. She was so tiny, weighing just three pounds and not feeding very well since she was taking nourishment from a feeding tube. Each day I watched for signs of Ella's improvement or decline. Would she soon come home with me, or would she leave us forever? I tried not to get too attached, but it was hopeless. Ella was a lovely child with a beautiful spirit that shone forth even then from her wide eyes and curious little face that seemed determined even then to stay with us for the immediate future.

Our little baby girl remained in the hospital for the next two months. While Ella appeared frail due to all the tubes and wires connected to her, I was never scared of her. She was really very handicapped, but I never thought of her in that way. All I saw when I stared into the hospital bassinette was a newborn child that needed and deserved the loving arms and attention of a mother who was eagerly waiting.

I was fortunate enough to be able to give up my teaching job and focus full-time on being a mother to little Ella. She needed attentive care, and I was happy to be able to provide it. Being able to care for this child in need met my own maternal need to feel useful and loved. Of course I already was those things in my marriage and to my now-grown daughters. But having a little one to hold, nurture, and care for summoned all my motherly instincts that I thought had been permanently packed away when Courtney had gone off to The University of Colorado. Bringing Ella into our home served as a rallying cause to bring our family together again. We would raise this baby as our own, despite each of our individual goals and aspirations. In a sense, Ella unified us in a new, dynamic way that made us closer and solidified our family interdependence. Of course, that meant we had to adjust our sails and set off in a new direction, but we were thrilled to have this unexpected opportunity that was unlike anything our family had ever previously experienced.

But our experimental course was not without challenges. It was hard to believe that such a beautiful child was not expected to live – and that was the most frightening part of all. We were going to bring her home as if we were a hospice care center. Our primary goal, the medical professionals reminded us, was to provide the small baby girl with comfort care. There would be no magical cures or reprieves. But our family's personal goal was to love this child as though she had been born to us biologically. In fact, it soon felt as though she could be our own child. Individually and collectively, we were determined to bond with her, and knew we would adopt her into our hearts as well as our lives.

Thinking back on my recent quest for adventure in my life following Courtney's departure for college, I decided to take another long, outdoor walk along a little dirt road in the mountains outside of Denver, not far from where we lived. It was a sunny day with a cool breeze, and I set off purposefully to think about my future and the prospect of bringing Ella home to live with us. This was not the new adventure I had been expecting. Had I been mistaken? Should I be preparing for some other type of event or experience to materialize? Immediately I brushed that thought from my mind. Ella had been brought to our notice for a reason. I began crying and pleading for some kind of sign as to what I should do, just as I had a short time before when I had longed for direction and a renewed sense of purpose.

It was so quiet out among the trees, the distant peaks glowing with sunlight. Birdsong broke into my thoughts occasionally, though all around me, everything else was quiet and serene. If only my thoughts could be like that!

I needed a sign, some indication that we had made the right choice in taking a badly-disabled infant into our family. We lacked experienced with disabled children, and it had been a long time since I had cared for a baby. What if it didn't work out? Please, please let there be a sign to confirm or confront our decision....

Looking up, I noticed a distinct cloud formation over-head. It appeared to be the image of an angel leading a small child by the hand, carefully pulling her along. Instantly I knew that Ella would indeed be my new purpose and adventure. My prayers had been answered – again!

With a sense of renewed peace in my spirit, I turned and went home, looking forward to Ella joining our family.

Somehow, all the details of organizing her release from the hospital and coming to live with us miraculously fell right into place. In a very short time we were able to bring our newest daughter home to live with us. We would love and care for her, and make this lovely young child as comfortable and secure as possible.

At that point, I didn't really ever think of her dying, although it was a great fear of my husband's. Looking back now, I guess I just trusted in whatever was going to be. I needed to believe she was going to be with us for the time being, and I trusted that would happen. If not, we would somehow adapt, though I tried not to think of that possibility. When Tom hinted at his dark fears, I would remind him that we were going to provide Ella with the best possible care and love that anyone could give her. I wasn't going to spend our valuable days together worrying about if or when. I was going to stay focused on the joy of having this little girl in our lives, come what may.

Chapter Five

Ella Joins the Family

When the exciting day came for Ella to be released from the hospital, we couldn't wait to bring her home. She was such a sweet baby, it seemed as though she had been made just for us, and we were convinced that no one else could take care of her as well as we were going to do. We would love her just as though she had been born into our family.

I have to admit our family life truly was turned upside down with Ella's arrival. There were so many instructions, medications, and tubes that it took my constant concentration to keep everything straight. Tom and I, along with the girls, went over all the instructions for Ella's care, which meant meeting her basic needs for food, sleep, cleanliness, and comfort. Yet, it was kind of fun to have a little one in the household again. She was so delicate and sweet, that we all enjoyed picking her up, holding, and feeding her, and caring for her in the way a family looks after any typical newborn.

This was all new for our three college girls, who were relatively close in age and had not had much experience with babies. They were excited to have Ella with us, and learned quite a bit about infant care while developing affectionate bonds with her.

At first we spent most of our time feeding the baby and trying to get her to eat. She was exceptionally cute, although her appearance was quite different from that of most newborns. Ella had a very tiny head. One side of her body was more developed than the other. She had been diagnosed with Schizencephaly, a syndrome that means she had large fissures or cavities in her brain. According to Schiz Kids Buddies (http://www.schizkidzbuddies.com/), a website that serves as a support group for more than 1,300 families with children that have this syndrome, Schizencephaly is a rare brain development disorder. Effects of the condition vary with each child. Typical problems can include developmental delays in cognition, speech, and vision, along with eating disorders. However, many of these kids have normal intelligence levels. Some have an abnormally small head, as did Ella, and possible hydrocephalus. Others can be mentally retarded with partial or complete paralysis and limited muscle tone. The reason schizencephaly can develop is the failure of normal neuron migration during the first five months of pregnancy. Possible causes include an in-utero stroke, gestational viral infections, and a gene mutation called EMX-2, which means normal nerve cell growth and migration do not occur, leading to the clefts or fissures in the brain. The syndrome can run in families, but it also can be seen initially in the newly-diagnosed child. Children are impacted in differing ways. The brain cleft may be unilateral or bilateral, open lip or closed lip, and is often connected to other brain disorders.

The best way to diagnose Schizencephaly is by MRI (magnetic resonance imaging).

Children born with this condition face an uncertain future. Depending on the size of the brain fissures, the child could have the same likelihood of living a normal lifespan as other children. But sometimes, the related medical issues can shorten a child's life. Each child may experience a variety of conditions that can impact their quality of life. Our family was determined to learn all we could to ensure that Ella received the most effective treatment and enjoyed a meaningful standard of living. For that to happen, we would have to educate ourselves about the syndrome and find support that could help us do everything possible to make Ella comfortable and happy.

In addition to this complex medical issue, Ella's optic nerve had not developed, so she was totally blind. She was destined to have seizures, and her brain activity would never progress beyond that of a three-month-old. Yet, she was physically in good condition. Ella grew slowly, but was extremely healthy – she was a survivor, with a buoyant will to live.

As we began looking for relevant information and learning more, we heard about a new program that was being put in motion in Denver's Children's Hospital, called the Butterfly Program. Basically, this was a home hospice program specifically designed for children and affiliated with the Children's

Hospital International Program for All-Inclusive Care for Children and Their Families. The program opened in 2002 as a collaborative effort between the Children's Hospital, the Children's Pharmaceutical Services (CPS), Centura Home Care and Hospice, and the Porter Foundation. Their goal was to provide supportive services and comfort care for children ranging from infants to young adults.

The death of a child is considered by many to be the most difficult bereavement a parent can face. The program's philosophy was to accept children with a life expectancy of twelve months or less and those with supportive/curative therapies, such as chemotherapy. They did not require the child to have a DNR (do-not-resuscitate) order in place upon enrollment. The program encouraged ongoing collaboration with the child's primary care physician and care team. Team members included a medical director, inpatient and outpatient coordinators, homecare and hospice nurses, chaplains, social workers, and a bereavement coordinator. Consultations were available for dietary needs, along with physical and occupational therapy. Also available were onsite seminars and occasional conferences on hospice and palliative care issues for families and caregivers.

We were fortunate to have this very special program available to us in Denver, not far from where we lived. Having no experience with caring for someone with significant developmental disorders, extensive disability issues, and palliative as well as hospice care, we were going to need help and support to do everything we could for our little Ella. I am so grateful we had the professional support and commitment of the Butterfly Program nearby for much-needed services and as an organization with wonderful people that we could call with questions or concerns as we covered unfamiliar ground.

The program and its staff were fantastic! A nurse came to our home every two weeks to examine Ella, adjust treatments and care, and answer our questions or provide guidance. A social worker also visited routinely, assisting us with issues related to social services, respite care, housekeeping support, and a host of other programs that prepared us to better understand Ella's condition and needs.

The doctor assigned to Ella at the Special Care Clinic of Children's Hospital was wonderful, a gentle man with great knowledge. He supported our goal of making Ella as comfortable as possible during what would presumably be the remainder of her short life. At that point it might be a matter of months, or perhaps a year or so.

With all the unexpected help coming alongside our family, the commitment we had made to Ella in that hospital room became even more manageable. Tom and I just looked at each other and smiled whenever someone would tell us about another service that was available to help us care for our baby girl. At the outset we had expected to care for Ella with few resources; now it became clear that help was available for just about any problem we might face.

"We made the right decision," I said to Tom one evening as I held the baby in my arms and smiled at my husband across the family room.

"Darn right," he smiled back over the top of the newspaper.

Chapter Six

Plans, Prayers, and Preparations

With our new routine finally settling into place, doing all we could to make Ella's life comfortable and secure, we weren't scared anymore about her dying. We just took it one day at a time, and one night at a time. (Did I mention we are old?) While it's true that having our sleep disrupted numerous times each night was not the fulfillment of our retirement dreams, we were a bit tickled about reliving our youthful parenting experiences. Yes, it was harder to lose sleep now, as our bodies were not quite as fresh and firm as they had been thirty years before. But in our journey through life we had gained something, too: we were more patient, more insightful, and more open to suggestions and help from others. At this midlife stage, we knew we didn't have all the parenting answers, in contrast to our youthful years when we had felt so much more confident in our ability to manage our children's needs. We didn't lack confidence now, but we were more aware of what we didn't know and had learned where to go for information. We were very proud of the help and support provided by our three daughters: Renae, Maureen, and Courtney, who lent a hand whenever possible between college classes and terms.

We also relied on our faith. We are a deeply spiritual family and believed that Ella's coming to stay with us had been ordained, and that we had somehow been selected to be her family for her sojourn on earth. Now we reminded ourselves to trust that something so powerful that had been put into place would find a way of working out to everyone's benefit. We had the will, so there must be a way!

Our unusual blend of parenting skills mixed with community support worked: To our delight, Ella grew and thrived. She appeared to be healthy despite her challenging medical issues. And she seemed truly happy. Holding a baby in your arms, you can just sense when they feel secure and restful. She was such a great child, so much fun and very cuddly, a roly-poly little girl that we enjoyed more and more each day. Thinking about my mid-life uncertainty about the various projects or goals I might pursue, I realized that we had been given the perfect "assignment' of caring for Ella; I could not imagine anything else being as rewarding or fulfilling.

Ella loved to be held and cuddled. She would snuggle against my chest like a little butterfly in its cocoon, waiting to be born. We kissed her down head, smooth face, and delicate fingers. Blessed with many hands and time each day to spend with her, Ella became the focus of our lives. She seemed to respond more intuitively than anyone had expected, and no one could believe it. Each month marked extra time she had been given to live on this earth with us, despite the doctors' initial prognosis that a child with her condition might not live long at all. Relatives, medical staff, and hospice workers were delighted by how well she was doing in our care, and we were unbelievably thrilled to have this baby in our lives. It may be hard to understand, but Ella gave us even more joy than we hoped we were giving her. Fragile and yet distinctive, her lovely eyes seemed to light up when any of us approached her or picked her up.

Yet, we tried to remind ourselves that Ella might not live to adulthood, and that her health might grow worse with time. The Butterfly Program and other social services helped us to understand and appreciate the nature of palliative care, which provides comfort rather than a cure, and may be able to help children with terminal illnesses to live well at every stage of their condition. We also learned that our family would now have psychological, spiritual, and social needs in bonding with Ella as well as preparing for the eventual separation. While we did not view palliative care as "giving up" on her treatment and longed-for recovery or extended life, we understood that palliative care addresses the current needs of a sick or disabled child, and that some children can receive curative care at the same time, though this was not the case with Ella.

Similarly, hospice care focuses on quality of life during the last months of life. Regulations limit hospice care to the last six months of life and exclude patients who are receiving curative treatment. Both palliative and hospice services can be provided at home, in a hospital, or in a private care facility.

We also began to understand that we would experience a grieving process as we bonded to Ella and she shared more of our lives. We were told to expect a normal range of emotions like frustration, despair, guilt, and anger, and that we should verbalize these feelings with each other, close friends or relatives, a support group, or even by writing in a journal. Holding strong, negative emotions related to fear and loss inside can not only make a person feel miserable, but also lead to stress-related illnesses like cancer, heart problems, and stroke. It was suggested that at some point, as Ella's condition deteriorated or when she passed away, we could get help from a professional grief counselor or join a support group for parents. The hospital or social worker would be able to help us find these services, if desired.

Caring for a severely-disabled child can drain the parents physically and emotionally. If others were to offer help, we were urged to accept it. Respite services were available if we found ourselves needing a break from the day-to-day work of meeting Ella's needs and keeping ourselves mentally and physically strong.

It was recommended that we learn about symptoms that appear as death approaches, like respiratory or bodily changes. Knowing what to look for would help us prepare for what was coming and allow us to be with Ella when the time came. Some professionals recommended that we made advance funeral preparations, including whether an autopsy might be necessary. Making difficult decisions like these in advance would help us to remain objective and provide quality time with Ella and each other at the time of her decease. We decided to defer these decisions until such time as medical opinion felt that Ella's health was deteriorating.

We were encouraged to spend time with our baby girl and simply enjoy each day, which was just the strategy we hoped to follow. We preferred focusing on the beauty of the moment rather than the sorrow that would come.

Caring for Ella of course involved more than holding and loving her. But that was the part we enjoyed most.

Chapter Seven

One Day at a Time

S trong-willed Ella continued to live and thrive, much to everyone's surprise and delight. In fact, she lived longer than anyone could have expected.

When she was a bit over a year old, she began having seizures. Fortunately, for the most part we were able to control them with medication and they were not life-threatening. But it was difficult to observe Ella in the throes of these events. At times she would become so frightened; she would wake up screaming and want to be cuddled, so we would bring her over to our big bed to keep her close for security and monitoring. We tried to make her as comfortable as possible at these times, though there was no way to explain to our little daughter what was happening to her, and that we were going to make sure she would be all right. We made a point of showing how much we loved her with hugs, kisses, and soothing her jerky movements with protective cuddling.

As the days grew on, so did our little girl. Our love grew, too. It was hard to believe such a tiny, developmentally disabled child could grasp such a meaningful place in our lives. I'm sure we couldn't have loved her any more deeply if she had been born to us naturally. Ella was good in her own unique way to fill our days with companionship, affection, and contentment.

Everyone cautioned us that she would not be around much longer – the doctors, nurses, experts, and even some friends. With her place secure in our hearts, it was hard to believe that this little angel would one day leave us in the not-too-distant future. We tried not to think about it, yet we understood that Ella was not destined to achieve adulthood; her death was just a matter of time. The thought of it just made our little girl all the more precious.

Maybe she sensed that her time on earth would be brief and tried to make each day special. Ella seldom cried or fussed. The exception to this was right before a major seizure, which mostly occurred at night. Ella would cry loudly as though anticipating what was to come. We took turns holding and comforting her, trying to soothe her fears away. It was hard; we needed sleep to be strong for her, and sometimes we had to do without it for long hours. But we did not begrudge Ella the best of our time, affection, and efforts. She deserved it all.

To make the best of our nighttime ventures, she wore a little t-shirt that said "Party in my room 2 a.m." It gave us a chuckle whenever she wore it and reminded us to celebrate the times we spent together, making the most of each day – or night.

Those sleepless nights were the most challenging part of Ella's care, with the crying, seizures, and lack of sleep. It was then that Ella became her most vocal and would even yell "hey," which was just a spontaneous reaction to her distress. Yet despite these difficult episodes, she really never seemed unhappy or uncomfortable. She actually set the example for us, showing us how to be patient and longsuffering. Ella displayed a tolerant attitude toward our clumsy efforts to assist her when in actuality we could do nothing to prevent or stop her seizures. Instead of uncontrollably screaming at us in criticism or complaint, Ella seemed to cling to us for whatever comfort could be gleaned from our touch and words.

Ella's world was dark due to her blindness, but I tried to be creative in teaching her about light – spiritual light, love light, comfort light – the types of "light" that she could not perceive on her body due to her inability to see, but hopefully felt deeply in her soul. The small child was scared and alone in her private world where the chaos of seizures could find her at any time, and she would struggle alone in her private darkness to understand what was happening to her body and mind as only an infant can do.

Of course, there was no purposeful way Ella could respond to her condition. She could only exist in her unique way as we strove to give her purpose and meaning in a world that was terribly scary and potentially unsafe. Fortunately, many types of seizures last just a few moments and gradually stop without medical intervention. The movements associated with seizures are caused by abnormal brain nerve cell activity, which can lead to unconsciousness, arm and leg rigidity, and facial or limb twitching. Parents who suspect their child is having a seizure should seek medical help for proper diagnosis and treatment. In general, it is important for parents to keep the child comfortable and away from any type of objects. Unless advised by the doctor, the child may not need to be restrained. Some children stop breathing for a moment or two, but typically they resume breathing on their own without medical intervention. Be sure to ask your doctor about this.

Many parents fear their infant will choke on its tongue, or bite it. The tongue cannot be swallowed, though it can sometimes fall back and block the airway. Rarely does a child severely damage the tongue. Do not place your fingers in the infant's mouth during a seizure. As seizure disorders can differ, it is always important to get a doctor's diagnosis and treatment plan rather than try to deal with the problem on your own.

We were fortunate in having plenty of medical advice and support for handling Ella's seizures and other complications. Although it hurt to watch her small body struggle with these episodes, we took comfort in knowing we were providing the best support available for her, and believed that no one could have given her more love or help than we did.

Caring for a special needs child is a monumental task that cannot be taken lightly. We learned that there is always more to learn about cases like these! Going through the painful experience of seizures and related problems with Ella, we grew to love her more each day and treasured the time she was part of our family.

Chapter Eight

Unconditional Love

Ella received our family's unconditional love, which seemed different from the affection Tom and I had given our own children. She was such a small, helpless child that we could hold nothing back and expected nothing in return.

Obviously at her age and in her present condition, Ella could do no wrong. Even if she had been able to get into mischief, I'm not sure how firmly I might have disciplined her. I felt she was guiltless, an innocent babe who had somehow reaped consequences she did not deserve. Of course, no one "deserves" to be born in that kind of brutal state. But there is a rare beauty, too, that is reserved for those who look so physically different from most people. Ella's small face appeared so pure that it seemed as though God had let us borrow her from Heaven for a short time to give us a glimpse of spiritual purity. Our daughter Maureen said, "She is an angel set among us." Each day led to stronger bonds with this fragile child who gave uncomplainingly of her love and dependence that immeasurably enriched our lives.

It didn't matter to us that Ella would never walk. We would never hear her speak. Nor would she ever be able to move her body of its own volition. Yet, somehow, Ella seemed "normal" to me. She went everywhere with us: out to dinner, to movie theaters, biking, skiing (in a carrier), and even roller blading! Her stroller was a tremendous resource as a braking device. She was never a hindrance to our family times and recreational activities. In fact, having Ella with us helped us to appreciate those times even more than before, when we realized that she would never be able to enjoy them the way we do. Making special arrangements to include her with us encouraged us to slow down and think through each activity and plan ways for Ella to participate. We tried to take her with us whenever possible rather than find a caregiver. Overall, she was surprisingly healthy, especially after she didn't have to receive oxygen anymore after we moved to a lower elevation. We were fortunate there were no special treatments or limitations required in caring for Ella, just a strict schedule that we followed carefully. She did not get colds, viruses, or fevers, but seemed to have a strong immune system despite her serious disabilities.

My husband and I gave ourselves grandparent names. His was "Beebo" and mine was "Nana," because people around us at the resorts, stores, skating parks, shopping malls, and restaurants would throw curious stares our way. I am sure they must have thought,

"Wow, what old people to have a young child. No wonder she is handicapped."

Anyone looking at us probably first noticed our gray hair and middle age. Although some couples do have children in their forties and fifties – especially nowadays with all the new technology to assist them – most of us are slowing down and sending grown children off to college, watching them launch a career, or helping to plan their weddings. Ella provided a refreshing change of direction for our lives.

I surprised myself with the strong maternal devotion I felt toward Ella, as well as our adult daughters. It was fun to dangle colorful toys over her chair and walk her around the house, singing in a low voice, and feeling her relax against me trustingly. I so much wanted to earn and protect her trust. The poor child had little else in her life; the least she deserved was security.

When friends young and old visited, they all wanted to play with Ella, hold her, or feed her. She was the center of attention and interest for everyone we knew. Often in public someone would give us a sympathetic look, but I wanted to point out that we were very happy with our baby, and their sympathy, while appreciated, could be saved for someone in greater need.

Having Ella in our home was like being given a new lifeline. It wasn't that our family life had been incomplete before. It's just that with our new addition, life became even fuller and more enjoyable. She was the adventure and surprise I had been expecting, and she fulfilled my expectations in ways I could not have begun to imagine. Young babies bring life into a home. No matter the quality of their existence, there is hope and fun and excitement. Nothing is dull or boring. Our daughters were amazed to observe their mother tend an infant, especially one as dependent as Ella. They had been too young and busy with their own lives to really notice how I had raised them. Now they could watch objectively as I cared for another child to whom I was as devoted as I had been to them.

"You're a great mom, Mom," Renae smiled one day while home on a semester break from the University of Kansas as she watched me rock Ella to sleep. "Need a break?"

"Not now, but thanks honey." She was a thoughtful girl who had become increasingly aware of her parents' needs as both she and we grew older. Renae also had a boyfriend with whom she seemed to be getting somewhat serious. I wondered if marriage and babies were on her mind.

"Babies are wonderful, but don't rush into anything before you're ready," I cautioned her, kissing Ella's soft hair.

"I won't," she smiled, heading for the door for her daily run. "But Ella makes me want to have one of my own someday."

"She's a sweetie," I agreed with a smile.

I was glad the girls were getting exposure to babies with special needs. You never know what life holds, and we had tried to prepare them for every possibility. Having Ella with us provided helpful insight and useful experience in many ways. Watching Renae close the door behind her, I felt a little sad at seeing how quickly she had grown up. She was

still in college, but it wouldn't be long before she graduated and was living on her own. I would miss her so much.
Thoughtfully I kissed Ella's head again, marveling at how
fast the years fly by.

Chapter Nine

Our Girls

While raising our three daughters, I made a point of teaching them that others' differences – physical or otherwise – should be accepted and not criticized. It's natural for young children to gawk at someone, young or old, who looks, acts, or speaks differently than observers are accustomed to. Even so-called "normal" people can display little quirks that kids quickly notice. Parents can put these "teaching moments" to good use by explaining how and why others may be different, and emphasize the need to accept everyone as equal as well as respect the obvious differences that can seem so foreign to young children.

Probably because of my teaching position, I was somewhat familiar and comfortable with kids with unusual disorders or physical and speech limitations that were enrolled in public school. Of course, students with more severe disabilities attended special education classes. Working with kids who looked or acted a bit different was part of my job, and

I had learned to admire the ways in which these students fought hard to overcome the disadvantages that made getting an education harder than for non-disabled students. I coached, guided, and assisted them in meeting their academic goals. Children with disabilities have always held a special place in my heart. They also taught me a lot. That is the perspective I shared with my girls during their growing-up years.

When Ella came to live with us, she taught my girls unconditional love – that every child is special, and that although she looked very different from other newborns, there was nothing "scary" about her. On their own Renae, Maureen, and Courtney saw the beauty in Ella, and was touched by the baby's courage in her struggle to survive, and her grace in everyday living.

Each of the girls developed an individual relationship with Ella. Our newest baby inspired them in various ways. They were so good with her, and openly showed their attachment to Ella in their frequent kisses and playful words. They learned from her to live in the moment and celebrate life however one could. She also taught them to appreciate each person's unique qualities and personal struggles.

In a more challenging way, they endured gracefully the quiet whispers and rumors:

"Whose baby is it, really?"
"What are they trying to hide?"

The girls were all of child-bearing age, and many people had heard of other families misrepresenting an illicit child as one they had adopted. Our daughters bore the gossip without embarrassment, denial, or complaint, or the need to justify Ella's origins or her disabilities.

A child is a child, and she was ours. We stood by her as a unified family without malice, resentment, or excuses. We were proud of Ella, and grateful to call her our baby.

Caring for a child – any child – requires patience. As any mother will agree, you have to arrange the family's activities around the baby's schedule of sleeping, eating, bathing, and napping. A baby that gets off schedule can get fussy, and that makes life tougher for everyone! Babies sometimes can be allowed to cry briefly as they wait for the next feeding or diaper change. A crying baby can get on everyone's nerves and upset the household, especially with visitors or guests around.

When a baby gets sick, it may require frequent monitoring for fever and medicine dosing. Sick babies often cry, and parents want to soothe them, taking time from other household duties and social opportunities.

In a busy household, a baby's needs have to come first, because an infant cannot wait to be fed, as adults can. Babies function more effectively when following a routine for consistency.

Renae, Maureen, and Courtney were learning these things every day. They were helping to raise a baby in our home, which gave them plenty of experience and observation time. This also allowed me to help them through my demonstrations and explanations. It really was a marvelous teaching opportunity. I almost felt as though I were back in the classroom some days!

More than that, caring for Ella as a family brought us closer together. We learned from each other when someone had a good idea to solve a new problem. I even learned some great tips from the girls, despite my having raised them! Sure, tempers flared at times, and someone's feelings got hurt on occasion if their suggestion didn't fly or if their schedule was disrupted by household adjustments. But more commonly, we discussed Ella's situation, her well-being, and our future. We shared worries and celebrated successes, like when Ella seemed to half-smile at one of us, though it may have been an involuntary gesture. Despite the fact the girls were mostly grown and had begun to go their separate ways through college toward the future, at home we came together as a team again to care for little Ella and to celebrate her life as a pivotal point for this new phase of family life. Who would have thought just months before that a new baby would come into our home and affect each of us profoundly?

Tom and I were proud of our girls – all four of them. Each was special in her own way, and added her own unique perspective to our family. As we watched our girls grow together as well as apart, I was grateful to have this very unusual opportunity in the person of baby Ella that molded us even more firmly as a family and taught us to rely on each other as never before. Ella became our guiding star that shone the light of love in our home to bring all of us together for a once-in-a-lifetime experience.

Chapter Ten

New Encounters

Because of our family's public excursions with Ella, we met so many people with stories to tell. It was like Ella was an angel magnet, attracting wandering souls who clustered around, eager to share their similar experiences.

Strangers would come up to us and say hello, or pass us on the street or in the mall. Seeing Ella, their faces would get animated and they would tell us their story. It was almost as if Ella had somehow conveyed her permission to explain their situation. Maybe it was because she was handicapped that they felt drawn to her. Given the time we had already spent with Ella as part of our family, we would understand the other person's need to discuss their background, almost as if Ella had somehow given them permission, being in public as she was. I wondered if some of them were ashamed of their disabled infant, nephew, or grandchild. We were like an extended family of unknown relatives, generally unaware of each other, yet secret members of our special association that only recognized each other when encountered in a public place. It was sort of like wearing a religious emblem, like a cross or star of David, and then seeing someone else wear one, you feel as though you share something important in common. Maybe a closer comparison would be a war survivor wearing a certain insignia meeting another survivor with a similar insignia or another marking to identify their shared background. You immediately sense a kinship and may decide to approach that person to explore it.

Ella's disabilities were her badge of honor. Because they were physical differences, hers were immediately recognizable and drew others who sympathized with or shared her plight via a relative or loved one. She was a soldier of sorts, a battle-scarred survivor who had braved the challenges of her newborn disabilities and had somehow defied the odds of her doctors predicting a brief lifespan. Here she was, many months beyond their predictions, and as anyone could see from looking at her, a child with serious challenges and yet a plucky spirit. She amazed many who saw her and drew from them corresponding stories of survival that you hear after a war.

Through encounters like these we met grandparents raising their grandkids, parents who had lost children, moms and dads of very sick kids, and those struggling with a wide range of physical and mental challenges. Sometimes their children were with them; at other times the child was in respite care or had passed away. Each shared their pain in touching accounts. I was surprised to see that all around us, people suffer and struggle every day, each with his or her own burden. Yet, many keep quiet for one reason or another, only unburdening themselves when they meet a fellow soldier in the trenches. A friend reminded me of Henry David Thoreau's famous quote:

"The mass of men lead lives of quiet desperation."
(Walden, 1851)

Ella intrigued passers-by in several ways. For one thing, she obviously looked different. With her small head and underdeveloped body, it was clear that something was seriously wrong. Of course when covered by a blanket and cap while outdoors, these differences were hard to see unless someone was close to her. But in the summer months or in an indoor place while uncovered, she could be seen clearly, and strangers often glanced at her, and then looked again, smiling with embarrassment before turning away. Medical employees, on the other hand, would shower her with compliments and attention:

"Look how cute she is!"
"I believe Ella looks like she's grown this month."
"Ella, you are getting to be a beautiful little girl."

Most of the comments were intended for us, her family, since Ella was so small and underdeveloped. We appreciated their concern and interest. Others asked to hold our baby, and would smile at her and kiss her tiny nose, which somehow I just knew Ella loved in some part of her limited consciousness. When passed from one set of arms to another, she would whimper briefly, as though she knew someone other than her family was holding her, and yet she kept her tears in check, seeming to realize the change in arms did not pose a threat. The doctors fell in love with her and praised our efforts in keeping her healthy.

"She looks so happy," one said following her physical examination.

"She is," I reassured him. "Ella is always like this. We are really lucky."

The doctor gave me a funny look as though to question my use of the word "lucky," since how could anyone raising a disabled child feel fortunate? But we did, and we hoped that other parents felt the same way toward their specially-challenged children.

During the holiday family get-togethers, our relatives cooed over our baby and took turns holding her, admiring her beautiful face and small limbs.

"She's just precious," my sister Nancy said, staring at Ella's sleeping features. "I remember when the other girls were little like this."

I was glad that she thought of all the girls as part of our family. Some relatives of adopted disabled children prefer to think of those children as apart, as those their bloodline could not have produced a child with problems. But our family was very warm and accepting. They understood our desire to give Ella the best quality of life possible. They gave us moral support and offered practical assistance when possible. Our holidays were extra fun when Ella celebrated with us.

Our daughters' friends were curious, too. "Look at her! She has the sweetest eyes," Courtney's friend Kate exclaimed on a Saturday when we went to visit our daughter on campus. Other dorm roommates crowded around and asked to hold Ella, many of them amazed at seeing close up and even handling a special needs child.

Ella made life more interesting for all of us, and I hope we did so for her, as well.

Chapter Eleven

New Directions

I have to admit that caring for Ella was a full-time joy as well as a full-time job.

While some caregivers of disabled children may feel deprived of the opportunity to live a normal lifestyle, I have met many who felt their lives had been blessed with the privilege of caring for a child with special needs. Naturally, our schedules and activities changed as we got used to the tasks associated with Ella's daily needs. But if she had not joined our family, we would have kept busy with other activities that most likely would have been far less meaningful. Ella enriched our lives in many ways. I never could have expected when we sent Courtney off to college that our days would change so dramatically. In some ways, it was like coming full circle from sending our last grown daughter off to college and then starting all over with an infant the age of Ella. But in another sense our lives now took a new direction with the unforeseen arrival of a special little girl who brightened our faces and our days.

We never got bored. Ella took me on many adventures! I learned to do many things that years before, I never would have imagined. Who would have thought such a tiny angel could have brought added excitement and meaning to our daily lives?

To meet state requirements of providing care for Ella's special needs, I had to become a Certified Nurse's Assistant (CNA). From many years of teaching experience and giving tests to entering the medical field and take temperatures, I was amazed by the dynamic medical world. My certification qualified Ella to receive Medicaid assistance, which was necessary for her many doctor appointments, tests, and procedures.

But as I learned more about becoming a CNA, I wondered if I could do it. Yikes, was I out of my element! A Certified Nursing Assistant provides assistance to people with healthcare needs, to those requiring help with activities of daily living (ADLs), and basic nursing routines (including bedside care), under the supervision of a Registered Nurse (RN) or Licensed Practical Nurse (LPN). The CNA accreditation is earned by demonstration the completion of the required workplace experience and academic study.

A Nursing Assistant provides routine care to patients so nurses can take care of more specialized functions for which they are qualified. A Nursing Assistant may perform tasks like preparing individualized care plans for patients, conducting nursing assessments, giving certain types of medications, and helping with surgery preparations. Students are trained to monitor patients' conditions and report to the nurse who is responsible. Typical duties of a CNA may include responding to patients' call signals, repositioning patients with little or no mobility (to prevent bedsores), observing patient conditions, measuring food and liquid intake and output, recording vital signs, and reporting to the supervisory staff. A Nursing Assistant also is trained to feed patients who cannot feed themselves, assist with walking or exercising, and help patients get in and out of bed (if they are able). Grooming assistance is taught as well to aid patients in bathing, shaving, dressing, or preparing for a procedure, treatment, or surgery, along with transporting patients by wheelchair or stretcher and changing bed linen as well as keeping the room clean. Sometimes test specimens must be collected for examination or testing by the doctor or laboratory.

Personally, a Nurse Assistant has to stay calm and understand as well as be able to implement appropriate emergency procedures.

The Omnibus Budget Reconciliation Act of 1987 (OBRA 1987) outlines federal nurse aide training regulations. State training programs are required to include a minimum of 75 hours, with 16 hours of supervised clinical training. Successfully completing this type of state-approved program leads to the certification of nursing assistants or what is sometimes called a State Tested Nurse Aid (STNA). Those who receive the certification are listed in the State registry of nursing aides. In order to maintain updated certification, nurse aides have to complete an additional 12 hours of continuing education each year.

Some Nurse Assistants are employed by hospitals and nursing homes. Others, like me, work with individual patients at home or on a freelance basis.

Although the program seemed demanding and time-intensive, I somehow felt confident about my ability to successfully complete the certification. I had to, for Ella's sake. The people I met in training were remarkable – both the teaching staff as well as other students. They seemed so caring and loving that I knew I had made the right decision to enroll in the CNA training.

While sitting through classes and then working with patients, I reflected on the serendipitous nature of this new phase of my life. At age thirteen I got a job – my first – working in a "Home" for severely handicapped children. I held that position through high school, and then influenced by my experiences there, I majored in Special Education in college.

Following graduation and teacher certification, I taught Special Education in Kindergarten and Preschool for thirty years before Ella came into my life. Who would have thought that all those years of my life had prepared me for the unique opportunity of caring for such a small, severely disabled child in my home? Now I could move her, feed her, and meet her daily needs using the best possible techniques for her comfort and safety.

A great friend, who was also Ella's physical therapist for six years, once told me as we were discussing our purpose in life that her beliefs were that your purpose will show up many times throughout your life, and that you just need to figure it out, whatever it is! Handicapped kids had been a significant part of my life since I was old enough to make decisions about what I wanted to do for a career. After several decades of doing a job that I really loved, I was now rewarded with the blessing of having a precious little girl like Ella to care for. Although the doctors had predicted her life would be brief and limited, I was determined to make her as happy and comfortable as possible. In return, Ella gave us many smiles and brought our family even closer together.

My training as a Certified Medical Assistant was just one of the many unexpected adventures that came about as a result of our love for little Ella.

Chapter Twelve

Happy Days

Ella continued to surprise us all. She was extremely healthy, not at all sickly as the doctors had predicted. In fact, Ella never got sick! Her cheeks were chubby and rosy, and her pretty dark hair grew shiny and thick. She was as beautiful of a baby as anyone could wish for.

It's difficult to condense the entire seven years of Ella's life with us. In fact, it's pretty unbelievable that the doctors initially gave her just a few months to live, and yet she astounded them by holding onto life and seeming to love each day. Her expression, while unfocused at times, could be peaceful, energized, and happy.

Each day was more or less similar. We greeted each other at the start of the morning. I could see the joy on her face – she loved being picked up and then hugged and kissed. Her features would light up, making us want to hold her even closer and play little word games with her that parents often do with infants and toddlers, like "Eensy weensy spider" and

"eye-winker, nose-dropper, mouth-eater, chin-chopper…"
and then tickle her chin!

We sang songs to her at bath-time; their rhythm and beat
was soothing or exciting, depending on the type of song. I
found myself remembering long-forgotten childhood lyrics
that I had sung to my older girls, and some I had heard from
my own mother. Ella would calm down as I began singing,
as though she absorbed the sound through my hands as well
as my voice. When I ran out of songs I switched to nursery
rhymes like "Humpty Dumpty" and "Little Jack Horner."
Sound and rhythm are important to children of all ages, even
those with sensory deficits. Singing made me feel cheerful,
too, and Ella must have felt that as I dried her off in a big
fluffy towel and dressed her for comfort.

Then there were the hours spent feeding her. After giving
up the bottle eventually, she ate really well, and I took care
to pick out the most tasty-sounding baby food I could find
to prepare nutritionally-balanced meals: fruits, vegetables,
meat blends, and desserts. Fortunately I had time – lots of
time – to spend with Ella, benefiting us both. There was no
need to rush or scramble, except for occasional appointments, and I tried to arrange these to be compatible with her
schedule so that she was well-fed and rested before venturing
out in the car. Our lives were in tune with her daily routine,
which remained fairly consistent, and that made it easier for
everyone.

In good weather we walked outside two or three times a
day, as the moving stroller was very soothing to her. I could
almost sense her feeling the cool breeze on her cheeks or

the warm sun kissing her face. Sometimes I varied our pace from a slow, ambling stroll to an invigorating spurt now and then, sharing the exhilaration of speed, at least momentarily. We might stop at a particularly peaceful or interesting spot, like where the geese flocked or near a beautiful flower garden, which I would tell her about as I "conversed" with Ella, describing the robins or cardinals we heard singing or describe the scenic or fragrant places we passed; I would mention the smell of pine trees or the fresh scent of spring flowers or freshly-cut grass. Usually it was just Ella and me, but sometimes one of the girls would come along, or we would stop to chat with the neighbors, who thought so highly of my little girl and praised her lavishly. It was a social time as well as providing fresh air and exercise (for me, anyway).

I dressed her in cute outfits that made her even more adorable. At first it was mostly onesies and sleepers. Later on she "graduated" to sweet little dresses and two-piece sets of shorts and top or shirt and pants. It was so much fun to dress her up and brush her hair, gently arranging her curls in little-girl styles that sent us running for the camera. Ella, too, seemed to notice at times that she looked especially cute, and would bask in our added attention.

At other times we spent hours cuddling in my favorite armchair rocker where I would read children's books aloud to her. She would get quiet as I read, as though taking it all in, and her small body fit neatly in my arms, her little legs wrapped snugly in her blanket, like a little frog. But she was more of a princess, often serene and contemplative, as though drawing life in and holding onto it for each day at a time.

Each day we thanked God for the wonderful events that we shared with this darling child and the sheer joy of having another day with her. Her life, being fragile, was precious. No one knew how long it would last, but we hoped she would stay with us forever. Each morning I reassured myself after careful inspection that she was as healthy as ever. Every evening I tucked her into bed with a kiss and a prayer. She came to represent a delicate piece of our family life that made us even more complete, now that she was a permanent part of our household. It was hard to remember what life had been like without her before, and none of us wanted to return to that state, as we were all growing deeply attached to this beautiful little girl.

Chapter Thirteen

Adjustments

Like other children, Ella did have cranky days, especially during her terrible twos and then four's, we called them! Most crankiness was associated with her seizure disorder and could be unpredictable in duration and intensity. All we could do anticipate periodic episodes and prepare with medical knowledge and training to respond in the most appropriate and supportive way. Of course, the seizures were hard on us all. It was disturbing to watch her small body shake and distort in an uncontrollable manner. I always wondered what she was thinking and how she felt. Did it seem like a natural, if unpleasant, part of her existence, or did she become emotionally upset without the ability to express her feelings to us? At least we were able to stay calm and soothe her in the prescribed way I had learned. Happily, many seizures passed quickly and Ella would seem unfazed by the transient episode, which gave me great relief. In time,

I got used to the seizures to a certain extent, but I was often sad and a little anxious when they occurred.

If she didn't sleep well or some little thing bothered her, Ella could fidget or fuss. But she never gave big tantrums. In fact, most of her discomfort would resolve fairly fast, and she would soon settle down into her normal good humor.

For the most part, Ella was what we thought of as perfect, truly a happy and beautiful little "pillow angel," as we called her, because when we placed her on a pillow or anywhere, for that matter, Ella stayed right there and didn't move. At least we didn't have to chase her all over the house when she reached the age that most children crawl or walk!

As our little girl grew, she changed from a beautiful little round infant to a longer version. She had lovely light brown curls – oh, so many curls, and dark blue, expressive, shining eyes. It was hard to remember she was blind. In fact, I never really thought of her as sightless. There were so many times when she seemed to drink in her surroundings with her entire face, eyes included, that I occasionally wondered if her vision might have slowly, miraculously, begin to develop. Intellectually I knew that was not possible, but emotionally I wanted to believe it, because Ella seemed so aware of everything around her that it was hard to imagine she could not see. I've heard it said that people with one type of sensory loss or limitation will have another sense that is extra strong; for example, someone who cannot see will have extra sharp hearing ability. Maybe that is how it was with Ella, that she could "hear" some of the things we experienced visually. Or maybe she had some type of sixth sense or intuition, as was thought by the ancients of those who were "touched by God" in a special way. While that may sound whimsical, anyone who knew Ella might consider such a thing possible. There was a look of "knowing" on her face at times that made her seem in tune with us all.

As mentioned in the previous chapter, Ella loved music of all kinds. It was calming to her, and I played it often as she grew. In addition to bath-time songs, I would play lullabies in her room at nap-time and bedtime, softly humming along so she could hear my voice and feel reassured and secure as she fell asleep. I imagined her thinking, "What a beautiful voice my Nana has." Relying much on voice and touch to interact with Ella, I was her constant companion and through me she experienced life vicariously.

I began to see life differently as well when I tried to view them as through Ella's eyes, had she been able to see. It had been a long time since I had held our daughters on my lap, bathed them, or sang to them, and getting back into a "mommy mindset" after several years was both challenging and rewarding. I felt my motherly responsibilities just as keenly as before, or more so, given Ella's unique condition. I tried to think of ways to make everyday activities interesting for her, just as any parent will do for a young child.

"That's the washing machine, Ella," I would say, flipping the dial to start a load of laundry. "Did you hear that? The timer says dinner is ready."

I could almost see the small wheels turning in her brain as she processed this information, and I would add details:

"Um, doesn't that smell good? You're going to love this warm peach puree."

Sometimes I lay in bed after Tom went to sleep and imagined myself to be like Ella. I lay very still, not moving, and closed my eyes although our bedroom was already dark since it was night. Slowly, very slowly I could "feel" sensory details that my eyes could not see and my hands were unable to reach and touch: the crickets beyond the open bedroom window, the sound of a light breeze ruffling the window blinds, and the faded scent of my husband's deodorant or my own freshly-shampooed hair. Without sight these impressions took on even greater meaning, and I decided from then on to be even more conscious about the ways I described these things to Ella.

Each day was a new journey that was oddly familiar and similar to past days, and yet distinctly different in its newness and possibilities. My creativity was frequently tapped to find ways of sharing daily experiences with our little Ella. As she grew, I hoped and felt that her sensory capabilities would expand, although the doctors told us this was unlikely. But I had great faith in my young daughter, and I would do everything possible to open pathways of communication and experience that she might not otherwise be able to access on her own.

Chapter Fourteen

The Magical "P"

Many people wonder why we called our little girl "Ella P." At first the "P" stood for "Pea," as in "Sweet Pea." Later we referred to her as our little "Peaberry," and then her nickname became just "Berry" since she was so sweet, and that name stuck for a long time. Often the "Berry" became "Bear," as in "Grizzly" when she was a crank. We were so playful with Ella that we gave her a variety of nicknames that were used for awhile and then forgotten, but the "P" stuck with her always.

As she grew a bit older, eventually "P" stood for "Princess." Ella was *our* little princess, and we were her doting subjects. It was fun to clothe her in those adorable ruffled dresses that little girls wear for special occasions like holidays and birthdays, and we would introduce her to our guests or in the homes where we visited in a joking way as "Princess Ella" is making her debut" or "The Princess Ella has arrived." All girls, of course, are their parents' little princesses, but our Ella made me think of the fairy tale "Cinder-Ella" who would one day claim her inheritance (a normally-developed body) and her kingdom in the next world, if not this one. Of course, our Cinderella was never mistreated like the storybook character. But Ella seemed to deserve so much more than she had been given from birth that it seemed right to hope and expect she would one day receive the gifts that would complete her, although in our eyes she was perfect just the way she was. Moreover, there was something magical about our Ella. She almost seemed fairy-like at times, as though she had been given to us for a special purpose. As time went on, we were amazed by the unique qualities of this beloved child to make us feel loved and values, even though she could never say so in words. With us, at least, Ella didn't need verbal language. Her expressive face conveyed all we needed to know.

Naturally, Ella had many, many "Ellaphants" – elephant-themed birthday parties. She was given books about elephants, she wore clothes with elephant patterns, and she even had music boxes decorated with miniature elephants. In effect, elephants became her signature symbol, and our family and friends celebrated many events by giving Ella a gift with this theme. Not only were elephants symbolic of our little girl because of their phonetic resemblance to her name, but also, ironically, the size and impact of these large creatures represented Ella's significance to our lives. Like the famous saying about ignoring the elephant in the room (meaning everyone is aware of an issue but do not speak of it), Ella's presence in our home had a similar effect. She had become such an important and natural part of our family that it seemed like she had been with us forever.

But the most important name change Ella received was the summer she turned six, and we adopted her, giving her our family name. Although there had never been any question that she was ours shortly after her birth, almost as if she had been born into our family, she now officially and legally became our daughter. Giving her our surname seemed a fair if inadequate exchange for the happiness she had brought us. We proudly introduced her as "Ella Geesey," although we had thought of her as sharing our family's public identity even when she technically didn't share our name.

The years had passed very quickly - too quickly. Already Ella had been in our lives for several years, but they seemed almost like weeks or months, as she had not changed physically in a dramatic way. Of course, she had grown somewhat, but not at all close to the size of a normal child her age. She was still the same size as a large infant, and we cared for her much like one in the way we bathed, fed, and transported her. I didn't really miss the fact that she was not growing up the way the other girls had. Of course when I thought about it, I felt bad that Ella was missing out on some valuable childhood experiences with school, friends, and even playtime. But as long as I felt she was generally healthy and content, I was satisfied with her progress and expected little change.

Reaching her sixth birthday marked Ella's rite of passage into what would have normally been her elementary school years. Instead of joining the local community by entering the educational system, Ella's birthday was quietly commemorated as her official membership into our family. I felt closer to her than ever before, more understanding of her needs and condition from the first six years of experience. I was eager to continue finding ways to clear Ella's path of obstacles so that her progression, however slight, could be made smoothly with my help as needed. Our family had grown deeply attached to this little girl, and we were devoted to her care and well-being. The adoption formalized by law our longstanding relationship that had been forged in love.

I was growing older, too, and yet caring for our little Princess kept me energized and enthusiastic. Renae, Maureen, and Courtney loved spending time with their young sister, talking to her, taking her places, and sharing anecdotes about Ella's escapades with them. I knew we had made the right decision to bring her into our family six years before, and I fervently hoped that we would be able to keep Ella with us for many more years to come. Everyone thought of her as our child; she legally had become our child. Surely we would be able to savor that relationship for years to come, having overcome so many difficult hurdles at the outset of her arrival and learning how to provide quality care and nurturing.

Chapter Fifteen

Preparing to Say Goodbye

There is an old myth that is probably told in many cultures of the world about the thread that is spun into each of our individual lives, comprising many strands. On the day that we die that thread is severed, cutting us off from this life and freeing us to discover the next. Some people's threads are cut suddenly by a car crash or a heart attack. But for others, the thread binding us to this world is cut gradually, one strand at a time, until the last one breaks. That is what happened with Ella.

Life is like a mountaintop. When you reach the pinnacle, the view is breath-taking and unforgettable, though you cannot stay up that high for very long. After a quick look around and a few moments of celebration, you begin the gradual descent, often more slowly and with greater difficulty than you made the climb. But for some, the descent occurs much more rapidly than the climb, and at an unexpected speed or manner.

We had celebrated our personal pinnacle of success with Ella's adoption. She had defied doctors' predictions for a brief survival and was now six years old, looking healthy and beautiful. She had molded comfortably within our family, and we could not envision a time without her in our lives. We had a comfortable routine, and Ella was doing better than ever.

But just when we were about to become complacent with her good fortune at having beaten the odds of her survival to this point, we began to notice that she was changing. At first my husband and I really didn't notice a dramatic difference, probably because we were with Ella all the time, and physical growth is not visually apparent right away, at least not usually to the caregivers that are around on a regular basis. But our girls popped in and out with frequent visits and soon noticed small differences that we had not yet grasped: Ella had begun to sleep for longer periods, with less waking time (no more partying at 2 a.m.). I would stare at her for several minutes at a time, waiting for her to wake up and continue our previous routine of eating, bathing, and playing. But she would just lie there unmoving, sleeping more and more as time went on. I wanted it to be a growth phase; all kids sleep more while growing. But instead of snapping out of it, she slept through most nights and off and on during the days. I had to admit to the girls that their observations were unfortunately accurate.

Then too, Ella was less verbal than she had been before. I missed her unique cooing sounds and various responses to my voice or other noises. As I carried her out in the yard we would hear a dog bark, which had grabbed her attention before. But now she did not seem to hear.

"Listen, Ella," I said excitedly, "hear the dog? He's barking at a cat."

There was no response or any kind of indication she had heard the dog or me.

But I was grateful that she still wanted to be held. She would nestle in my arms and rest peacefully there, as if that was the only thing that mattered. As she dozed more often, and then eventually most of the time, I would study her face with its delicate eyelids, faintly veined, covering her lovely eyes all too often. Her skin seemed a bit paler, and she didn't move around as much as before. It was like she was settling in for the inevitable destiny that was waiting, try as I might to ignore it or scare it away.

Finally Tom and I could see Ella's form growing larger and more distorted in obvious ways. Now all the signs that we had missed before – perhaps because we hadn't wanted to see them - were coming distinctly into focus and could not be denied. Even our relatives and neighbors noticed.

Ella's body became longer and leaner. She was no longer the plump, infant-like child we were accustomed to. Her appearance began to look more handicapped as her disabilities became increasingly prominent. Her body was not equipped to handle such radical changes. Ella's little bones began to bend and grow crooked, unable to sustain her enlarging body. With these obvious changes that must be acknowledged, I became truly alarmed; surely this was a temporary phase or a change in her condition that would right itself, and Ella's growth would slow down and let her body adjust to its new proportions rather than put added stress on her frame. Maybe the doctors could prescribe some kind of treatment or medication that would slow the process, or perhaps surgery could be scheduled to help her bones adapt to her changing form, although the doctors had never mentioned such an option. Desperate to calm my growing anxiety and convince myself and others that Ella was not changing *that* rapidly, I latched onto any theory or possibility – along with some impossibilities – to explain away the physical changes in her body and behavior that we were forced to confront.

Outsiders noticed her changing appearance right away. Strangers in stores or at the mall stared much more than they had done in the past, and their looks of pity broke my heart. Their expressions told me far more than Ella's reposing features that something was not right. Children that we encountered during our daily strolls would pass by and glance at her with curious expressions, or they would stop and stare in fascination. Ella looked "different." How could I explain why to them? As they asked me questions or made offhand comments, I noticed Ella's facial expressions would change if she were awake; she loved hearing children's voices and babies crying. But all too often now, she slept through more of these sounds and our once-loved walks together, although they had previously been the high points of her day.

Although I had successfully cared for her all these years with great love, Ella was beyond my ability to help her now. All I could do was prepare for the inevitable and continue to keep her comfortable and secure.

Chapter Sixteen

Facing the Inevitable

W hat would I do if Ella left us? How would I survive? I began to cherish every day even more. I guess, deep down, we had known that Ella would not be with us forever. But to actually face the future without her seemed unthinkable.

My life had been carefully wrapped around this little girl for seven years. Each day that came and went was planned with Ella's schedule in mind. She had become a permanent part of our family, a beloved daughter to Tom and me, and a sister to our three older girls. Our extended family loved her.

We had planned our old age with Ella as a big part of it. There was so much we wanted to share with her, to teach her, and to enjoy with her. There were trips to take, events to attend, and activities to do. Ella had become so entrenched in our lives that it was impossible to imagine the future without her.

The fact of Ella's demise was made transparently clear when a visiting nurse asked me if I was prepared for my daughter's death.

My breath was sucked from my lungs – I couldn't breathe. Of course I wasn't prepared; how could you ever prepare for such a tragic event?

I cried often, sometimes alone and other times with Tom or the girls. Occasionally I would break down in the most unexpected places, like a restaurant when I would see a little girl, apparently healthy, who reminded me of Ella. But our Ella was not going to get well. She would never improve. In fact, she was dying a little bit each day, and nothing I could do would stop that.

Cradling Ella in my arms, I studied her face over and over, imprinting her features permanently in my mind as future memories. I waited for her eyes to open and gave her the most welcoming smile I could muster. I kissed her hair, her face, her small hands, holding her close, transmitting my love through the curve of my arms. She seemed to sense my deep emotion and settled comfortably into my embrace.

I prayed for more time. Surely she could live a little longer, maybe until scientists invented some new way to prolong her life and cure her of the disabilities that were now claiming her strength. Or maybe she could live just long enough for me to fully come to terms with her passing. Then I realized how selfish I was. I wanted Ella to live for my happiness, overlooking the fact that each day might be growing increasingly difficult for her.

Then I couldn't help thinking each day might be her last. What would I do? How would I react? How would Tom, Renae, Maureen, and Courtney respond? How could a person just stand by and wait?

I suppose we went through the usual grief-and-dying process outlined by Elizabeth Kubler-Ross. First, there was denial. Ella's nurse must be mistaken. Surely not all patients die when their medical caregivers indicate the end is near. Despite her sleepiness and lethargy, Ella might rebound and come back as strong as before, or stronger. Maybe she was going through a weak phase. Our Ella just looked too healthy to be at death's doorstep.

But watching her body become weaker and frailer, something told me she really was slipping away from us. So the second stage of grief hit me full-force: anger. I am not a wrathful person by nature; I seldom raise my voice or maintain a grudge. But a deep-seated edginess inside me began to rear up: Why did Ella have to die? Wasn't it enough she had been stricken with a disability all of her short life, that she had been shortchanged of the physical senses and mental development that most of us are blessed with? Why did she have to die so young as well? We had adjusted to each other so well over the years; she was a perfect fit with our family. It wasn't fair that we had tried so hard to meet her needs and make her content and secure, and it still wasn't enough to keep little Ella on this earth. Why did some people suffer so much, and others, seemingly so little? Why did we have to give up this dear child that we loved so deeply?

Then sadness swept over me. Ella would never play with a puppy, go to school, attend graduation, pursue a career, fall in love, get married, have children and grandchildren, own a home, or celebrate any of life's meaningful rituals as part of a family or as a self-fulfilling individual. Her time was up; there would be no opportunities, no hope, and no achievements. I tried to view her leaving us from the other perspective as well: Ella would never have her heart broken, experience a car accident, suffer a loss, or be abandoned. Nor would she suffer abuse or know hunger. But those thoughts were cold comfort.

Finally, there was resignation. I could do nothing to save Ella; no one could. Her approaching death was one of life's mysteries and sorrows. Other parents had lost children, and our loss would be similar – unthinkable, unbearable. A child should never have to die, but we don't make the rules, only watch them carried out by unseen forces.

Slowly I began to realize we had been blessed to keep Ella with us as long as we had. Doctors had expected this outcome many years before, shortly after her birth. But Ella had defied their predictions and survived to enjoy life to the fullest of which she was capable. In addition, she brought our family unanticipated joy and surprising depth of love. She was unique, and we had benefited from knowing and loving our precious little girl.

Chapter Seventeen

Practical Concerns

Losing a child must be the most grievous sorrow on the face of the earth. There is no other like it. To watch a little one suffer, linger, and then fall away, like an autumn leaf from its parental tree, is heart-breaking. This depth of loss, which often seems so senseless and needless, changes a person. You will never be the same. We didn't exactly understand that as we prepared for the end, however. Somehow working through the four stages of grief, I realized we had to make some practical decisions that were very difficult, and yet completely necessary.

In coming to terms with our imminent loss and sorrow, I was forced to deal with some personal issues. One was guilt. Had I done enough for Ella? Was there more I might have done to prolong her life or make her more comfortable? Or had I allowed myself to get too close to her, to become too attached, knowing that Ella's time with us was going to be short? I thought back on the times, few as they had been, when I had vacuumed the rug or done laundry before playing with Ella or taking her for a walk. Realistically, these chores had to get done. But now I was second-guessing myself; had there been times when I should have put Ella first at any cost? Rationally I reminded myself that she had been the focus of my life for seven years, and that I had given her quality time each day. Truthfully, there could be no regrets in that area.

Then I wondered if I should have taken her to the doctor more often, or less often. Maybe she would have healed naturally if I had just let nature take its course. But again, I had to remind myself such worries were illogical. Our home, the household environment, Ella's care, and even my attitude had been all that it could be; in all honesty, there was nothing we could have done more for her. I had to stop looking for someone or something to blame.

Instead, I had to keep myself busy making the practical arrangements. Ella might pass away any day now. What would I do when that day came?

Hard as it was, we needed to plan Ella's funeral and burial. Counselors will advise you not to wait until the person passes away to make final arrangements, as most people will be distraught and perhaps not thinking clearly. By contacting the appropriate sources, I was able to learn some of the most important things to consider when planning a funeral, which after all, is for the survivors, not the deceased. Here are a few things to keep in mind.

Select a funeral home service and director in your area, preferably one with experience in arranging children's services. The director will discuss your wishes and help you make decisions regarding the public calling hours, the funeral service, and the cemetery plot.

Choose the cemetery plot in a preferred cemetery location. Keep in mind the fact of whether you plan to visit the cemetery from time to time.

Select the burial coffin and vault, or urn. Some grieving families pay high amounts for these items due to an emotional response in anticipating a loved one's death. Try to be objective as you consider costs.

Consider purchasing or at least selecting the headstone or marker for the gravesite, along with the writing and any designs you want to have placed on it. Some people choose just the person's name and dates, while others select engraved patterns or images, as well as possible verses or Scriptures.

Pre-plan the burial clothing. Choosing the outfit beforehand makes it easier than waiting to do it later.

Though not necessary to do in advance, you may want to think about the type of family floral arrangement you might want to order for the coffin.

Determine the church or site of the funeral service, along with any religious official that you wish to provide a eulogy. Check with the clergy to see if he or she performs this type of funeral eulogy.

Plan the funeral service, including the type of eulogy, music, readings, and tributes. If someone you know performs suitable vocal or accompaniment music, it's a good idea to ask if that person would be willing to participate in the funeral service.

Write an obituary and select the news media that you want to carry the announcement. Although a funeral director or staff member can assist with this, you may want a family member to prepare the announcement to ensure accuracy and a personal touch.

Plan the after-funeral arrangements, such as a church dinner or family reception time. Often a church or social organization to which the family belongs will plan this commemorative meal, but it might be a good idea to check ahead of time and find out for sure. Although it may seem cold and unemotional to plan the funeral ahead of time, doing so will make the actual events go smoothly for everyone and take the immediate pressure off family emotions at the time of passing.

When a parent learns that a child is in the terminal stage of illness, it is prudent to learn everything possible about what to expect at the end stage of the disease. Of course, every child is different, and sometimes things don't turn out as expected. But in many cases there are symptoms to watch for and report to the nurse, which can also prepare the parents and family for the child's imminent demise. Ask the child's doctor or nurse about expected changes in the child's physical condition, such as respiration, heart rate, skin texture and temperature, etc. There may be other signs to observe as well.

Taking control of these practical matters empowers an otherwise powerless parent to feel as though she or he is doing something practical to maintain the child's comfort and well-being. It is horrible to just watch a small child slip away, but keeping active keeps the mind busy and bolsters a person's spirits. Often, doing something – anything – will restore calm to a parent's frantic mind.

But we were faced with inescapable waiting. Day after day, hour after hour, our watching intensified. I scanned her face and studied her movements for signs of change. But there was no clear way to know exactly what Ella was going through. She just slept more and moved less. I checked her routinely, around the clock if not more frequently. Each morning when I got up, I headed for Ella's crib to see if she had made it through the night. At night before going to bed, I stood by her side and watched her sleeping features, wondering if she would make it through the night without me there beside her. And I continued to pray.

Chapter Eighteen

Going Home

From the point of the nurse's question and our response in making the dreaded preparations, the days passed too quickly, each one filled with deepening love, sorrow, and hope that somehow the inevitable would be delayed. The only positive aspect of our waiting was that we had time to prepare ourselves mentally and emotionally for what was to come. We cherished Ella all the more, even as she responded to us less and less.

Would it be today? Tomorrow? This weekend? Next week?

But I knew we could not live this way, thinking each day might be her last, that any change we noticed might be a sign of the end. We had lived with her and loved her too long; it wasn't right to simply wait around like this, dreading the worst. I tried not to think of "the end," but rather tried to see each day as a new beginning, a time to appreciate even more fully Ella's uniqueness, her gentle personality, her beautiful expression, and all that she had meant to us.

One day about four months later I woke up and saw immediately that something was wrong.

Getting up as I usually did, I went into Ella's room to check her. Before, she had often been stirring before I was, or at least starting to awaken. But on this day she was so sleepy. When I tried to gently rouse her, she would not really wake up. She wasn't herself.

Stifling my panic but with tears falling, we hurriedly got ready and took Ella to her doctor's office for evaluation. He quickly examined her and rushed us to the Emergency Room, where another examination by the staff led to their calling the director of the local "Butterfly Program."

The Butterfly Program is a multi-faceted service for families with terminally ill children. We had registered long before, and now it was time to ask for their assistance. We were told what to expect, which was similar to what I had already learned on my own over the previous few months: signs and symptoms of the body's gradual shutting down, the opportunity to comfort our child and ease her transition, and our own preparation for the end.

All I could do was pray "Thy will be done" as I held Ella close to me, cuddled frog-like in my arms. Although I knew God's will probably wasn't what I would have chosen, I acknowledged the need to accept the inevitable and submit to His divine plan for Ella. I understood that God loved my child as much as I did, or more. Everything was now in His hands, and we patiently accepted His will.

A few years before, a close friend had told me to keep those special words close: "Thy will be done" when my father was dying. They had helped me then, and were a source of great comfort now. It was all we had to cling to.

Ella's doctor was summoned. He had been expecting the call after sending us to the Emergency Room earlier. But he was in shock, as she had never been sick in nearly seven years. No one had really expected her life to ebb in this manner. He expressed regrets at this turn of events, and offered to help us in any way possible, should the need arise. But there was nothing he could do for Ella.

Our nurse remained with us a long time that day. She was very kind and caring, and serendipitously, she had an elephant tattoo on her neck that showed just below the hairline of her perfect short haircut. Sensing our helplessness and pain, she offered to sit with Ella while we used the restroom or stepped out for a break. She also monitored Ella's vital signs and bodily functions, which confirmed that our little girl would not be with us much longer.

The Butterfly Program works to keep families together and to meet care needs as they arise in the terminal phase. Thankfully, the program arranged to let us – our three girls included – take Ella home. We took turns cuddling and holding her, kissing her face, patting her arms, and stroking her hair. Ella became stiller as the hours wore on, as though the peace that had accompanied her nature all her short life was now preparing to encompass her completely in death. There would be no seizures or struggles, only a deeper rest than Ella had experienced before now as she settled into comfortable repose and her expression completely relaxed.

We lost track of the time. All of us sat together in the room with Ella, watching her, talking softly, recalling special memories since her earliest days with our family. She had brought us all closer, which was especially meaningful after the girls had all gone away to college and came home only on holidays and semester breaks. Ella had been bonded us and held us together in united affection for the little stranger who had become one of us.

Now, almost seven years later, it was impossible to let her go. How could we continue on? It was as if a piece of our family was chipping off and would forever bear the scar from the permanent break.

Ella, our little star, was about to find her own special place in the universe. The earth had been too small for her beauty and grace, and now we would share her with Heaven and the angels. That thought gave us comfort.

But we were still heartbroken when we glanced at her still form lying in my arms as she took a slight breath and passed on. It was so faint that we could not tell for sure she was gone until we stared at her unmoving chest and shadowed features for several seconds and discerned the unwanted truth, that Ella had left our home for a much grander one and was in better Hands than ours.

Chapter Nineteen

Shadows and Starlight

O vercome by grief, I left the house and walked briskly around outside, crying in the dark, for most of the night. Knowing our area was relatively safe, Tom and the girls let me go, although they would look out from the window sometimes to be sure they kept me in view. They knew how much Ella had meant to me, and what it cost to let her go. I wept and wept, hardly paying attention to where I was going except to follow the sidewalk down our block and back again. The night was clear, and the moon was nearly full, making it bright enough to see my way without stumbling, though I hardly looked.

Hundreds of memories flooded into consciousness, all fraught with emotion. I recalled the many times Ella and I had walked this path together, me talking and pushing her stroller, and she seeming to strain to experience everything along the way. I remembered the wind tousling her hair and the neighbors stopping to say how pretty she looked.

Recalling my baby's expression and the fun we had shared, I wondered how I would ever be able to take a stroll without her again. I passed the tall fir tree where I had pointed out a cardinal singing its heart out one morning. There was our neighbor's fence that was clustered with daisies and sunflowers. Of course, in the dark I couldn't see these things, but I could envision them in my mind, in the secret place full of memories that Ella and I had shared.

Hearing our front door open a time or two, I knew Tom was checking on me to be sure I was all right. But they understood what I was going through; they had loved Ella too, though I had been closest to her. The girls and Tom had seen how close Ella and I had become over the years that had flown by too quickly. Only now was I beginning to realize that I had needed her as much as she had needed me. What would I do without her?

I kept moving up and down the road like a ghost in the dark, sobbing quietly and trying to pray.

"God, why did you take our little angel so soon? I wasn't ready for her to leave us."

"But she was ready," the wind seemed to whisper as it blew through the spruce, fir, and pine trees all along the street. The branches waved gently up and down, as though offering their own brand of sympathy. I thought of the times I had explained the wind to Ella, brushing my fingers across her cheek as she flashed a delighted smile. The crickets chirped lightly as I passed as if to share their own memories of our special strolls along this path. In the forested slopes at the end of the street I heard an owl, a mournful sound that only brought more tears streaming down my cheeks.

It was chilly. I had to go inside. But I was still miserable and desperately needed to find Ella out here where we had spent so many wonderful times together. Our spirits had truly bonded in the majestic beauty of the nearby mountains. Pausing before our house, I stared into the night sky, which was clear and bright, filled with a million distant gems of light. Surely a sight like this had greeted Ella's soul as it left her frail body to soar toward the stars. I wondered if one of those twinkling lights above was her spirit on its way to meet her Creator where she would be received with great love.

Tranquility bathed my senses. There was an ethereal feeling in the air, a transcendent quality that helped me to feel Ella's presence far above. With a great sigh I turned and headed for our front porch.

Just as I approached the steps I heard a bell tinkle.

The sound was so surreal, so quiet. The wind had died away, and yet – a bell. I thought of the Christmas movie with its joyous and playful reminder:

"Every time a bell rings, an angel gets her wings."

Peace poured over me like warm water on a cold day. I felt Ella wrap her little arms around me. It was her turn to comfort.

A moment later I darted up the steps and into the house.

Somehow we made it through the next few days. You know how it is when someone dies; you stumble through each day's schedule like a zombie, sometimes feeling nothing, and other times screaming inside with the pain of loss. I tried not to look at her bed too often, or pick up her toys. When I did, I would remind myself to stop after a few seconds so the pain wouldn't become unbearable. Renae and Maureen were quiet, like me, but Courtney tried to cheer us up and handled many of the errands and tasks that needed done when the rest of us didn't feel like it. Tom was quiet, too, patiently waiting for my grief to subside. He would hold me close at night, and I loved his presence beside me. But no one could replace Ella in our home or my heart.

On the day of Ella's memorial service, we were driving along without saying much, looking at the familiar surroundings as we made our way toward our destination. Suddenly we saw beautiful, billowing clouds overhead and then Maureen gasped.

"Look Mom!"

I didn't have to ask what she meant. Against the deep blue sky as background, the fluttery clouds had formed a trail of perfect little elephants, holding trunks, dancing their way across the sky. Elephants had always been Ella's signature symbol.

She was with us! She was that angel that had been set among us! The clouds were a joyful reminder for each of us to be aware that we sometimes entertain angels who minister to humans in their time of need....

Chapter Twenty

Making Peace

Our world was severely rocked by Ella's death. The pain for me was so intense, it cannot be explained. The days and months that followed were heart-wrenching as we gave away Ella's equipment, knowing another disabled child could use these things.

Having Ella with us brought about life-altering changes. She had impacted every bit of my being – my entire outlook on life. It's surprising to realize that a young child, especially a disabled one that cannot function normally, could have such a dynamic effect on a person and a family.

I had been through the grief process many times before, having lost parents, a sibling, and friends. But nothing could describe the pain of losing a child – Ella had been our child, and would always be our child.

Again, as during the most critical phases of Ella's brief life, we relied on many others for strength. We were very fortunate to be surrounded by many who willingly and lovingly helped us and were very generous – neighbors, coworkers, friends. There were also people we knew very little but who had heard of Ella from others or in some way had been connected with her care. Everyone was so kind and giving in ways that surprised and touched us. We were especially blessed by the support of the Butterfly Hospice Program. They knew just what to say and how to answer our questions or provide advice.

Soon after Ella's death, a neighbor quietly said, "I am so sorry for your loss."

Her little girl, also named Ella, looked up at the mother and asked, "Mom, what did she lose?"

The question made me smile, and then later I thought about it: What did I lose?

I lost a love of my life,

My joy for living,

A big piece of my heart,

And my desire to move on.

But I didn't lose my faith. Although the pain of missing Ella is almost unbearable, I have unwavering faith, not an understanding of why, but a belief that I will be whole again someday.

We take each day, one at a time, just as we did when Ella was with us. There are no promises, no certainties, and no guarantees in life. Each of us is given just the moment at present, and we must embrace it fully before it, too, is gone forever.

I thank God for every second I had with Ella. I could not have imagined a better adventure or personal journey, although we are now, as Henry David Thoreau once surmised, living in "quiet desperation."

*****

Heading up the mountain slope on that chilly December late afternoon, I looked toward the lonely headstone that cast a surprisingly long shadow for such a small child's legacy. My thoughts drifted to Ella's beautiful face as I watched the colorful pinwheel that we carried spin in the cold mountain air.

I miss you.

Carefully we placed our gifts on Ella's grave, stepping forward one by one to set there a bouquet of flowers, a small ceramic bunny, and the pinwheel.

I wish you boundless love, peace, and joy on your first Christmas in Heaven, my little angel. We look forward to being with you again one day.

Acknowledgments

To RMC with all my love,

Tom – my heart and soul

Debra – for understanding my vision

Nancys' – for all your wise words and love

KLC – for true friendship

Thanks for being in my life!!

CPSIA information can be obtained
at www.ICGtesting.com
Printed in the USA
LVHW09*2352220818
587775LV00015B/427/P